Object-Oriented Programming with C++

A Fundamental Guide to Building Robust, Scalable Applications with Real-World Examples

COPYRIGHT

Copyright ©2024 All Rights Reserved

No part of this publication may be reproduced, distributed, or transmitted in any form or by any means, including photocopying, recording, or other electronic or mechanical methods, without the prior written permission of the publisher, except in the case of brief quotations embodied in critical reviews and certain other noncommercial uses permitted by copyright law.

DISCLAIMER

The author and publisher have made every effort to ensure the accuracy and completeness of the information contained in this book. However, they assume no responsibility for errors, inaccuracies, omissions, or any other inconsistencies herein. This book is not intended to provide legal, financial, or other professional advice.

Contents

COPYRIGHT	2
DISCLAIMER	3
Chapter 1: Introduction to Object-Oriented Programming (OOP)	16
Conclusion	23
Chapter 2: Getting Started with C++	24
Conclusion	35
Chapter 3: Understanding Classes and Objects in C++	36
Conclusion	48
Chapter 4: Inheritance in C++	49
Chapter 5: Polymorphism in C++	64
Conclusion	77
Chapter 6: Encapsulation and Data Hiding in C++	78
Chapter 7: Inheritance in C++	92
7.7 Summary	108
Chapter 8: Polymorphism in C++	110

Chapter 9: Abstract Classes and Interfaces in C++ 121

Chapter 10: Exception Handling in C++ 131

Chapter 11: Templates in C++: Generic Programming 140

Chapter 12: Standard Template Library (STL) in C++ 150

Chapter 13: Exception Handling in C++ 163

Chapter 14: Design Patterns in C++ 174

Chapter 15: Best Practices for Object-Oriented Programming in C++ 190

Chapter 1: Introduction to Object-Oriented Programming (OOP)

1.1 What is Object-Oriented Programming?

Object-Oriented Programming (OOP) is a programming paradigm centered around the concept of "objects," which represent real-world entities or concepts. These objects contain data (referred to as attributes or properties) and behavior (referred to as methods or functions). This approach allows for a more organized and modular way of writing code, making it easier to manage, understand, and extend.

In OOP, four core principles govern how software is designed:

Encapsulation

Abstraction

Inheritance

Polymorphism

These principles help in creating applications that are scalable, reusable, and maintainable. By focusing on real-world "objects," OOP helps model complex systems more intuitively than procedural programming.

1.2 The Four Pillars of OOP

Let's briefly explore these pillars:

Encapsulation: This is the process of bundling data (attributes) and methods (functions) that manipulate the data into a single unit, or class. It also involves restricting direct access to some of an object's components, which is crucial for protecting data integrity. Only certain functions are allowed to access and modify data, creating a well-defined interface for interacting with an object.

Example: In a banking application, customer data like account balance is encapsulated within the class. The user can check or update the balance only through specific methods (e.g., deposit() or withdraw()), preventing accidental or unauthorized modification.

Abstraction: This concept involves simplifying complex systems by hiding unnecessary details and showing only relevant information. It helps in focusing on the essential functionalities without getting overwhelmed by the underlying implementation.

Example: A "Car" class might expose methods like start(), drive(), and stop() without needing to show how the engine or transmission works internally.

Inheritance: Inheritance allows one class to acquire the properties and methods of another class, promoting code reuse and logical hierarchy. A derived (child) class can inherit from a base (parent) class, and even extend or modify its behavior.

Example: A "Vehicle" class might serve as the base for a "Car" class and a "Motorcycle" class, both of which inherit general vehicle properties like speed, but might have specialized methods unique to their type.

Polymorphism: Polymorphism allows objects of different classes to be treated as objects of a common superclass. It enables one interface to be used for a general class of actions, making the code more flexible and extensible.

Example: Both the "Car" and "Motorcycle" classes might have a startEngine() method. Polymorphism allows these different objects to be interacted with in a uniform way while executing different implementations of the method.

1.3 Procedural Programming vs. OOP

To better understand the value of OOP, it's helpful to compare it to procedural programming, the more traditional style of writing code where instructions are executed in a sequence.

In **procedural programming**, the focus is on functions that manipulate data. As the program grows larger, this approach can lead to issues like code duplication and difficulties in managing complexity. Changing one part of the system can cause a ripple effect, requiring changes in many other parts.

In contrast, **OOP focuses on the entities or objects** that the program interacts with, each having well-defined attributes and behaviors. This leads to a more natural mapping between the real world and the program, reducing complexity and promoting modularity.

1.4 Advantages of Object-Oriented Programming

The key advantages of OOP include:

Modularity: Code is organized into separate classes and objects, which can be independently developed and maintained.

Example: You can work on a "User" class without affecting the "Transaction" class, even though both might interact in the final system.

Reusability: Code can be reused across different parts of a program or even in other programs. Inheritance and polymorphism make it easy to extend existing functionality without rewriting code from scratch.

Example: If you have a "Payment" class, it can be reused in multiple projects with little or no modification.

Scalability: OOP allows developers to build larger and more complex applications in a systematic way. As the application grows, adding new features or modifying existing ones is easier because the system is built around modular, independent objects.

Example: A large e-commerce platform can have modules for users, products, orders, and payments, each represented by a class. These modules can be worked on separately, and features can be added without breaking the entire system.

Maintainability: OOP code is generally easier to maintain and modify. Since functionality is grouped into objects, finding and fixing bugs or making changes is more straightforward. The principles of encapsulation and abstraction also make it easier to understand how different parts of a system interact.

Example: If you find a bug in how discounts are applied in an e-commerce platform, you can go straight to the "Order" or "Cart" class to investigate, without worrying about how other parts of the system work.

1.5 The History of C++ and OOP

C++ was developed by **Bjarne Stroustrup** in the early 1980s as an extension of the C programming language. It was initially called "C with Classes," and the primary goal was to add OOP principles to C while maintaining the power and flexibility that C provided.

The development of C++ was driven by the need for a language that could efficiently handle both system-level programming (like C) and high-level abstraction, allowing for more complex applications to be built. Over the years, C++ has become one of the most widely used languages in industries such as game development, embedded systems, financial applications, and more.

C++ combines the low-level control of system resources typical of C with the object-oriented paradigm, offering the best of both worlds for many types of applications.

1.6 Real-World Applications of OOP

OOP is widely used in software development across various industries, making it a critical skill for developers. Some real-world applications include:

Game Development: Games are often built using OOP principles. Each game element, such as characters, objects, and scenes, can be modeled as separate classes. C++ is particularly popular in game development because of its performance and OOP capabilities.

Example: In a game, a base "Character" class might define general attributes (e.g., health, speed), while specific classes like "Player" or "Enemy" inherit from it.

Enterprise Software: Large-scale applications like Customer Relationship Management (CRM) and Enterprise Resource Planning (ERP) systems are often built using OOP. Each part of the system, like "Customer," "Order," and "Inventory," can be treated as an object, making the system more manageable and scalable.

Example: An "Order" class can manage all aspects of customer purchases, while a "Customer" class handles customer details.

Graphical User Interfaces (GUIs): GUI development in OOP allows each graphical component (like buttons, windows, and menus) to be treated as objects with their own attributes and behaviors. This makes it easier to build and modify complex user interfaces.

Example: In a GUI application, a "Button" class can have properties like size, color, and behavior (what happens when clicked), and new buttons can be created by instantiating objects from this class.

Conclusion

Object-Oriented Programming with C++ offers a robust and scalable approach to software development by organizing code around objects and the principles of encapsulation, inheritance, abstraction, and polymorphism. Understanding these foundational concepts is the first step toward mastering OOP and using C++ to build powerful, maintainable applications.

In the next chapter, we'll dive into the basics of C++ syntax, exploring how to set up your environment and write your first C++ program.

Chapter 2: Getting Started with C++

In this chapter, we will explore how to set up a C++ development environment, understand basic C++ syntax, and write your first program. By the end of this chapter, you'll have a solid foundation for building C++ applications.

2.1 Setting Up Your Development Environment

Before we dive into writing code, it's essential to have a proper development environment set up. Here are the basic tools you'll need to write and run C++ programs:

Compiler: A C++ compiler translates the code you write into machine code that your computer can understand. Popular C++ compilers include:

GCC (GNU Compiler Collection): Available on Linux, macOS, and Windows (via MinGW).

Clang: An alternative to GCC, also widely used on Linux and macOS.

Microsoft Visual C++: Included with Microsoft Visual Studio and is commonly used on Windows.

IDE (Integrated Development Environment): An IDE helps you write, edit, and debug your code with features like syntax highlighting, code completion, and debugging tools. Some popular IDEs for C++ development are:

Visual Studio (Windows): Comes with a built-in compiler and debugger.

Code::Blocks: A free, open-source IDE that works on Windows, macOS, and Linux.

CLion: A cross-platform IDE by JetBrains with powerful tools for C++ development.

VS Code (Visual Studio Code): A lightweight editor that supports C++ through extensions.

Text Editor (for lightweight development): If you prefer a simple text editor and don't need all the features of a full IDE, you can use editors like:

Sublime Text

Atom

Notepad++

Setting up GCC on Windows (using MinGW):

Download and install MinGW (Minimalist GNU for Windows) from mingw.org.

Add MinGW to your system's PATH environment variable so that you can use g++ commands from the command line.

Test the installation by opening a terminal and typing g++ --version.

Setting up Visual Studio:

Download and install Visual Studio from Microsoft's website.

During installation, select the "Desktop development with C++" workload to install all the necessary C++ tools.

2.2 Basic C++ Syntax: Data Types, Variables, and Operators

Once your environment is ready, let's begin by exploring some core elements of the C++ language. These form the building blocks for writing any C++ program.

Data Types

C++ provides several built-in data types that you can use to store information. These include:

Integers (int): Whole numbers (e.g., 5, -100)

Floating-point numbers (float, double): Numbers with decimal points (e.g., 3.14, -2.718)

float: Single precision

double: Double precision (more accurate than float)

Characters (char): A single character (e.g., 'a', 'Z', '1')

Booleans (bool): Represents truth values (true or false)

Strings (std::string**)**: A sequence of characters. C++ supports strings through the Standard Template Library (STL).

Variables

In C++, variables are used to store data. A variable must be declared with a specific data type and optionally initialized with a value. For example:

cpp

```cpp
int age = 25;          // Integer variable
float temperature = 36.5;  // Float variable
char grade = 'A';      // Character variable
bool isPassed = true;  // Boolean variable
std::string name = "Alice"; // String variable
```

Operators

C++ provides a variety of operators to perform operations on variables:

Arithmetic Operators:

Addition (+), Subtraction (-), Multiplication (*), Division (/), Modulus (% for remainder)

Example:
cpp

```
int a = 10;
int b = 5;
int sum = a + b;   // sum = 15
int product = a * b; // product = 50
```

Relational Operators: Compare values.

Greater than (>), Less than (<), Equal to (==), Not equal to (!=)

Logical Operators: Used to form logical expressions.

Logical AND (&&), Logical OR (||), Logical NOT (!)

Example:
cpp

```
bool result = (a > b) && (a != 0);  // result = true
```

Assignment Operators: Assign values to variables.

Simple assignment (=), Addition assignment (+=), Subtraction assignment (-=)

2.3 Writing Your First C++ Program

Now that you're familiar with basic syntax, it's time to write and run your first C++ program. We'll start with the classic "Hello, World!" example.

cpp

```
#include <iostream> // Preprocessor directive

int main() {  // The main function
    std::cout << "Hello, World!" << std::endl;  // Output text
    return 0; // Return statement
}
```

Let's break down the code:

`#include <iostream>`: This is a preprocessor directive that includes the `iostream` library, allowing us to use input/output operations like printing text to the console.

`int main()`: This defines the `main()` function, the entry point of any C++ program. Every C++ program must have a `main` function.

`std::cout << "Hello, World!"`: This line prints "Hello, World!" to the console. The `std::cout` object is used for output, and `<<` is the insertion operator, which directs the text into `std::cout`.

`return 0;`: This signals the end of the `main()` function. Returning 0 indicates that the program ended successfully.

Compiling and Running the Program

Once you've written the program, the next step is to compile and run it.

In GCC (command line):

Save the program as `hello.cpp`.

Open a terminal and navigate to the folder where hello.cpp is saved.

Run the following command to compile the program:
Copy code
```
g++ hello.cpp -o hello
```

If no errors occur, run the program:
bash
```
./hello
```

In Visual Studio:

Create a new C++ project.

Write the program in the code editor.

Click "Build" to compile and "Run" to execute the program.

2.4 Basic Input and Output in C++

C++ uses the `cin` object for input and `cout` for output, both of which come from the iostream library.

Using `cout` for Output

We've already seen `cout` in the "Hello, World!" example. Here's another example:

cpp

```cpp
#include <iostream>

int main() {
    int age = 25;
    std::cout << "I am " << age << " years old." << std::endl;
    return 0;
}
```

This will output:

css

```
I am 25 years old.
```

Using cin for Input

To take input from the user, use cin. Here's an example:

cpp

```cpp
#include <iostream>

int main() {
    int age;
    std::cout << "Enter your age: ";
    std::cin >> age;
    std::cout << "You entered: " << age << std::endl;
    return 0;
}
```

When this program runs, the user is prompted to input their age, and the entered value is stored in the age variable.

2.5 Control Structures in C++

Control structures allow you to control the flow of your program based on conditions.

If-Else Statements: This structure is used to execute code based on a condition.

cpp

Copy code

```cpp
int number = 10;
if (number > 5) {
    std::cout << "The number is greater than 5" << std::endl;
} else {
    std::cout << "The number is less than or equal to 5" << std::endl;
}
```

For Loop: The for loop repeats a block of code a certain number of times.

cpp

```cpp
for (int i = 0; i < 5; ++i) {
    std::cout << "Iteration: " << i << std::endl;
}
```

While Loop: A while loop keeps executing as long as a condition is true.
cpp

```cpp
int i = 0;
while (i < 5) {
    std::cout << "Iteration: " << i << std::endl;
    ++i;
}
```

Conclusion

This chapter introduced the basics of C++ and how to set up a working environment to write your first program.

Chapter 3: Understanding Classes and Objects in C++

In this chapter, we'll dive deeper into the foundational concepts of **classes** and **objects**, which are the core of Object-Oriented Programming (OOP). By the end, you'll understand how to define classes, create objects, and interact with them in C++.

3.1 What are Classes and Objects?

In C++, **classes** and **objects** are the primary tools used to model real-world entities and their behaviors.

Class: A class is like a blueprint or template that defines the attributes (data) and behaviors (functions) that an object can have.

Object: An object is an instance of a class. When you create an object, you are creating a specific instance that follows the structure defined by the class.

Think of a **class** as the blueprint for building a house, and an **object** as a specific house built using that blueprint. You can create many houses (objects), but they all share the common structure and features defined by the blueprint (class).

Class Example

Consider a class that models a **Car**:

cpp

```
class Car {
public:
   std::string brand;
   std::string model;
   int year;

   void drive() {
      std::cout << "The car is driving" << std::endl;
   }
};
```

This Car class has **three attributes** (brand, model, and year) and **one behavior** (the drive() function). Now, we can create objects based on this class.

Creating an Object

To create an object, you simply instantiate the class like this:

cpp

```
Car myCar;
myCar.brand = "Toyota";
myCar.model = "Corolla";
myCar.year = 2020;

std::cout << "My car is a " << myCar.year << " " << myCar.brand << " " << myCar.model << std::endl;
myCar.drive();
```

This code creates an object myCar from the Car class, assigns values to its attributes, and calls its drive() method. The output will be:

csharp

My car is a 2020 Toyota Corolla
The car is driving

3.2 Defining Classes in C++

In C++, a class is defined using the class keyword followed by the class name and a set of curly braces {}. Inside the class, you define **attributes** (also called **member variables**) and **methods** (also called **member functions**).

Access Modifiers

Classes in C++ can have attributes and methods that are either:

Public: Accessible from outside the class.

Private: Accessible only from within the class.

Protected: Accessible within the class and its derived classes (used mainly with inheritance, which we will cover in a later chapter).

By default, class members are private. Here's an example:

cpp

```cpp
class Person {
private:
    std::string name;
    int age;

public:
    void setName(std::string personName) {
        name = personName;
    }

    void setAge(int personAge) {
        age = personAge;
    }

    void introduce() {
        std::cout << "Hi, my name is " << name << " and I am " << age << " years old." << std::endl;
    }
};
```

In this Person class, the name and age attributes are **private**, meaning they cannot be directly accessed or modified from outside the class. Instead, we provide **public** methods setName(), setAge(), and introduce() to interact with the object.

3.3 Creating Objects and Accessing Class Members

Once you've defined a class, you can create **objects** to represent real-world entities. Let's use the Person class as an example.

Creating an Object and Accessing Public Methods
cpp

```
Person person1;
person1.setName("Alice");
person1.setAge(30);
person1.introduce();
```

This code creates an object person1, sets the values for name and age using the public methods setName() and setAge(), and then calls introduce() to display the information.

The output will be:

csharp

Hi, my name is Alice and I am 30 years old.

3.4 Constructors and Destructors

A **constructor** is a special member function that is automatically called when an object is created. It is used to initialize objects and can be overloaded to provide different ways of constructing objects. A **destructor**, on the other hand, is a function that is called when an object is destroyed, typically used to release resources.

Constructor Example

cpp

```
class Car {
public:
    std::string brand;
```

```cpp
    std::string model;
    int year;

    // Constructor
    Car(std::string carBrand, std::string carModel, int carYear) {
        brand = carBrand;
        model = carModel;
        year = carYear;
    }

    void displayInfo() {
        std::cout << "Car: " << brand << " " << model << " " << year << std::endl;
    }
};
```

Here, we define a constructor for the Car class that takes three parameters (carBrand, carModel, and carYear) to initialize the attributes of the class when an object is created.

cpp

```cpp
Car car1("Tesla", "Model 3", 2023);
```

```
car1.displayInfo();
```

The output will be:

```yaml
Car: Tesla Model 3 2023
```

Destructor Example

A destructor is defined using the ~ symbol followed by the class name. It's typically used to clean up resources such as closing files or freeing memory.

```cpp
class Car {
public:
    std::string brand;
    std::string model;
    int year;

    // Constructor
```

```cpp
    Car(std::string carBrand, std::string carModel, int carYear) {
        brand = carBrand;
        model = carModel;
        year = carYear;
    }

    // Destructor
    ~Car() {
        std::cout << "Destroying the car object: " << brand << " " << model << std::endl;
    }
};
```

When an object of the Car class goes out of scope, the destructor is called, and the following message is displayed:

csharp

Destroying the car object: Tesla Model 3

3.5 The this Pointer

In C++, every object has access to its own address through a pointer called this. It's implicitly passed to all member functions and can be used to refer to the object's own members.

Using this in a Class

cpp

```cpp
class Person {
private:
    std::string name;

public:
    void setName(std::string name) {
        this->name = name;   // 'this' refers to the current object
    }

    void introduce() {
        std::cout << "Hi, I am " << this->name << std::endl;
    }
};
```

In the setName() function, this->name refers to the member variable name of the current object, while name refers to the parameter passed to the function.

3.6 Static Members of a Class

In C++, a class can have **static members**, which are shared among all objects of the class. Static members exist independently of any objects, and they are accessible using the class name.

Static Variables Example

cpp

```
class MyClass {
public:
    static int count;

    MyClass() {
        count++;
    }
};

int MyClass::count = 0;  // Initialize static member
```

```cpp
int main() {
    MyClass obj1;
    MyClass obj2;

    std::cout << "Number of objects: " << MyClass::count << std::endl;
    return 0;
}
```

Here, the count variable is shared by all objects of the class, and it keeps track of how many objects are created. The output will be:

javascript

Number of objects: 2

3.7 Constant (const) Members

In C++, you can make a member variable or member function **constant** by using the const keyword. This means that the variable's value cannot be changed, or the function cannot modify the object's data members.

Constant Member Function Example

cpp

```cpp
class Car {
private:
    std::string brand;

public:
    Car(std::string carBrand) {
        brand = carBrand;
    }

    void getBrand() const {  // This function cannot modify any data members
        std::cout << "Brand: " << brand << std::endl;
    }
};
```

Declaring a member function as const ensures that it does not modify any of the object's data members.

Conclusion

This chapter covered the foundational concepts of **classes and objects**, which are at the core of object-oriented programming in C++. You now understand how to define classes, create objects, and use constructors, destructors, and other key features like the `this` pointer and static members.

In the next chapter, we will explore **Inheritance**, a powerful feature that allows you to create new classes based on existing ones, promoting code reuse and modular design.

Chapter 4: Inheritance in C++

In this chapter, we will explore one of the key principles of Object-Oriented Programming (OOP): **inheritance**. Inheritance allows you to create new classes based on existing ones, promoting code reuse and enabling more efficient application development. By the end of this chapter, you'll understand how inheritance works in C++, the types of inheritance, and how to apply them to real-world scenarios.

4.1 What is Inheritance?

Inheritance is a mechanism in C++ by which a new class (called a **derived class**) can acquire the properties and behaviors of an existing class (called a **base class**). The derived class inherits all the members (attributes and methods) of the base class, while also having the ability to add new members or modify existing ones.

Example of Inheritance

Imagine you have a base class Animal and you want to create a more specific class Dog:

cpp

```cpp
class Animal {
public:
    void eat() {
        std::cout << "This animal is eating." << std::endl;
    }
};

class Dog : public Animal {
public:
    void bark() {
        std::cout << "The dog is barking." << std::endl;
    }
};
```

In this example, Dog is a derived class that inherits from the Animal base class. The Dog class can access the eat() function from Animal and also define its own function bark().

cpp

```
Dog myDog;
myDog.eat();  // Inherited from Animal
myDog.bark(); // Defined in Dog
```

The output will be:

csharp

```
This animal is eating.
The dog is barking.
```

4.2 Types of Inheritance

C++ supports several types of inheritance, which determine the relationship between base and derived classes. The most common types are:

Single Inheritance: A derived class inherits from only one base class. Example:

cpp

```cpp
class Bird : public Animal {
    // Inherits from Animal
};
```

Multiple Inheritance: A derived class inherits from more than one base class. Example:

cpp

```cpp
class Swimming {
public:
    void swim() {
        std::cout << "This animal can swim." << std::endl;
    }
};

class Fish : public Animal, public Swimming {
    // Inherits from both Animal and Swimming
};
```

Here, Fish can both eat() (inherited from Animal) and swim() (inherited from Swimming).

Multilevel Inheritance: A class can be derived from another derived class, creating a chain of inheritance.
Example:
cpp

```cpp
class Mammal : public Animal {
    // Mammal inherits from Animal
};

class Cat : public Mammal {
    // Cat inherits from Mammal, which in turn inherits from Animal
};
```

Hierarchical Inheritance: Several derived classes inherit from a single base class.
Example:
cpp

```cpp
class Cat : public Animal {
    // Cat inherits from Animal
};
```

```cpp
class Dog : public Animal {
    // Dog also inherits from Animal
};
```

Hybrid Inheritance: A combination of more than one type of inheritance, typically involving multiple and multilevel inheritance. This type is complex and rarely used in practice.

4.3 Access Control in Inheritance

C++ provides three levels of access control for inheritance, which determine how the members of a base class are accessible in a derived class:

Public Inheritance: Public and protected members of the base class remain public and protected in the derived class, respectively.
cpp

```cpp
class Base {
public:
    int a;
protected:
```

```cpp
    int b;
private:
    int c;
};

class Derived : public Base {
    // a remains public
    // b remains protected
    // c is inaccessible
};
```

Protected Inheritance: Public members of the base class become protected in the derived class, and protected members remain protected.
cpp

```cpp
class Derived : protected Base {
    // a becomes protected
    // b remains protected
    // c is inaccessible
};
```

Private Inheritance: All public and protected members of the base class become private in the derived class.

cpp

```
class Derived : private Base {
    // a and b become private
    // c is inaccessible
};
```

4.4 Constructors and Destructors in Inheritance

When a derived class object is created, the **constructor** of the base class is called first, followed by the constructor of the derived class. Similarly, when the object is destroyed, the **destructor** of the derived class is called first, followed by the destructor of the base class.

Base and Derived Class Constructor Example

cpp

```
class Animal {
```

```cpp
public:
    Animal() {
        std::cout << "Animal constructor called." << std::endl;
    }

    ~Animal() {
        std::cout << "Animal destructor called." << std::endl;
    }
};

class Dog : public Animal {
public:
    Dog() {
        std::cout << "Dog constructor called." << std::endl;
    }

    ~Dog() {
        std::cout << "Dog destructor called." << std::endl;
    }
};

int main() {
```

```
    Dog myDog;
    return 0;
}
```

The output will be:

kotlin

```
Animal constructor called.
Dog constructor called.
Dog destructor called.
Animal destructor called.
```

As you can see, the constructor of the base class (Animal) is called before the constructor of the derived class (Dog), and the destructors are called in reverse order.

4.5 Function Overriding

Function overriding occurs when a derived class provides a new implementation for a function that is already defined in its base class.

The function in the derived class **overrides** the one in the base class.

Example of Function Overriding

cpp

```cpp
class Animal {
public:
    virtual void makeSound() {
        std::cout << "The animal makes a sound." << std::endl;
    }
};

class Dog : public Animal {
public:
    void makeSound() override {
        std::cout << "The dog barks." << std::endl;
    }
};
```

In this case, the `makeSound()` function is overridden in the `Dog` class. If we call `makeSound()` on a `Dog` object, it will use the overridden version:

cpp

```cpp
Dog myDog;
myDog.makeSound();  // Output: The dog barks.
```

Virtual Functions

To ensure that the correct version of a function is called when dealing with inheritance, especially when using pointers or references, C++ uses **virtual functions**. When a function is declared as `virtual` in the base class, it ensures that the version in the derived class is used if it exists.

cpp

```cpp
Animal* animalPtr = new Dog();
animalPtr->makeSound();  // Output: The dog barks.
```

Here, even though `animalPtr` is of type `Animal*`, the `Dog` version of `makeSound()` is called because `makeSound()` is a virtual function.

4.6 The `final` and `override` Keywords

override: Ensures that a derived class is actually overriding a base class function. If the base class function does not exist, the compiler will generate an error.
Example:
cpp

```cpp
void makeSound() override {
    std::cout << "The dog barks." << std::endl;
}
```

final: Prevents further inheritance from a class or function overriding in derived classes.
Example:
cpp

```cpp
class Dog final : public Animal {
    // No other class can inherit from Dog
};

void makeSound() final {
    // No derived class can override this method
}
```

4.7 Multiple Inheritance and the Diamond Problem

C++ allows a class to inherit from more than one base class, but this can lead to the **diamond problem**, where a derived class can inherit the same base class multiple times through different paths.

Example of the Diamond Problem

cpp

```cpp
class Animal {
public:
    void makeSound() {
        std::cout << "Animal sound." << std::endl;
    }
};

class Mammal : public Animal {
    // Inherits Animal
};

class Bird : public Animal {
    // Inherits Animal
};
```

```cpp
class Bat : public Mammal, public Bird {
    // Inherits both Mammal and Bird, but both have Animal as a base class
};
```

The `Bat` class inherits `Animal` twice (once via `Mammal` and once via `Bird`), causing ambiguity. To resolve this, C++ provides a mechanism called **virtual inheritance**.

Virtual Inheritance Example

cpp

```cpp
class Animal {
public:
    virtual void makeSound() {
        std::cout << "Animal sound." << std::endl;
    }
};

class Mammal : virtual public Animal {
    // Virtual inheritance of Animal
};
```

```cpp
class Bird : virtual public Animal {
    // Virtual inheritance of Animal
};

class Bat : public Mammal, public Bird {
    // Inherits Animal only once
};
```

With virtual inheritance, Bat will have only one instance of the Animal base class.

Chapter 5: Polymorphism in C++

In this chapter, we will explore the concept of **polymorphism**, one of the four pillars of object-oriented programming (OOP). Polymorphism allows objects of different classes to be treated as objects of a common base class, enabling a single interface to represent different types. This chapter will cover both **compile-time** and **run-time** polymorphism, including function overloading, operator overloading, and virtual functions.

By the end of this chapter, you will have a solid understanding of how polymorphism promotes flexibility and scalability in C++ applications.

5.1 What is Polymorphism?

Polymorphism, derived from the Greek words "poly" (many) and "morph" (form), means that the same function or operation can take on different forms. In C++, polymorphism allows you to write more generic and reusable code, as it enables objects to be processed differently based on their data type or class.

There are two types of polymorphism in C++:

Compile-time Polymorphism (Static)

Run-time Polymorphism (Dynamic)

5.2 Compile-Time Polymorphism

Compile-time polymorphism occurs when the decision to bind a function call to its definition is made at compile-time. This is primarily achieved through:

Function Overloading

Operator Overloading

5.2.1 Function Overloading

Function overloading allows multiple functions to have the same name but with different parameter types or numbers of parameters. The compiler determines which function to call based on the argument types passed to the function.

Example:

cpp

```cpp
#include <iostream>
using namespace std;

class Printer {
public:
    void print(int num) {
        cout << "Printing an integer: " << num << endl;
    }

    void print(double num) {
        cout << "Printing a double: " << num << endl;
    }

    void print(string text) {
        cout << "Printing a string: " << text << endl;
    }
};

int main() {
```

```cpp
    Printer myPrinter;
    myPrinter.print(5);        // Calls print(int)
    myPrinter.print(4.5);      // Calls print(double)
    myPrinter.print("Hello");  // Calls print(string)
    return 0;
}
```

In the example above, the function print() is overloaded three times to accept an integer, a double, and a string. Based on the type of argument provided, the appropriate version of the function is invoked.

5.2.2 Operator Overloading

Operator overloading allows you to redefine the behavior of operators for user-defined data types. This is particularly useful when you want operators like +, -, ==, or << to work with objects.

Example:

cpp

```cpp
#include <iostream>
using namespace std;
```

```cpp
class Complex {
private:
    double real;
    double imag;

public:
    Complex(double r = 0, double i = 0) : real(r), imag(i) {}

    // Overload + operator
    Complex operator + (const Complex& other) {
        return Complex(real + other.real, imag + other.imag);
    }

    void display() {
        cout << real << " + " << imag << "i" << endl;
    }
};

int main() {
    Complex num1(3.5, 2.5);
    Complex num2(1.5, 3.5);
```

```cpp
    Complex result = num1 + num2;   // Uses overloaded + operator
    result.display();               // Output: 5 + 6i
    return 0;
}
```

Here, the + operator is overloaded for the Complex class to perform addition on complex numbers. Without operator overloading, you would need to write a specific method to perform this operation, but overloading makes the code more intuitive.

5.3 Run-Time Polymorphism

Run-time polymorphism occurs when the function that will be called is determined at run-time rather than at compile-time. This is mainly achieved through **virtual functions** and **pointers to base class** objects.

5.3.1 Virtual Functions

In C++, a **virtual function** is a member function in a base class that can be overridden in a derived class. It allows a derived class to provide a specific implementation of a function that is declared in the base class. Virtual functions enable **dynamic dispatch**, which means the decision of which function to invoke is made at run-time based on the object type.

Example:

cpp

```cpp
#include <iostream>
using namespace std;

class Animal {
public:
    virtual void makeSound() {  // Virtual function
        cout << "Animal makes a sound" << endl;
    }
};

class Dog : public Animal {
public:
    void makeSound() override {  // Overrides the base class function
        cout << "Dog barks" << endl;
```

```cpp
    }
};

class Cat : public Animal {
public:
    void makeSound() override {
        cout << "Cat meows" << endl;
    }
};

int main() {
    Animal* animalPtr;
    Dog dog;
    Cat cat;

    animalPtr = &dog;
    animalPtr->makeSound();  // Output: Dog barks

    animalPtr = &cat;
    animalPtr->makeSound();  // Output: Cat meows

    return 0;
}
```

In the example, makeSound() is declared as a virtual function in the Animal class and is overridden by the Dog and Cat classes. When we assign the pointer animalPtr to objects of Dog or Cat, the correct makeSound() function is called based on the actual object type, even though the pointer is of type Animal*.

5.3.2 Pure Virtual Functions and Abstract Classes

A **pure virtual function** is a virtual function that has no implementation in the base class. It is declared by assigning 0 to the virtual function in the base class. A class that contains at least one pure virtual function is called an **abstract class**, and it cannot be instantiated directly. Derived classes must provide implementations for all pure virtual functions.

Example:

cpp

```
#include <iostream>
using namespace std;

class Shape {
```

```cpp
public:
    virtual void draw() = 0; // Pure virtual function
};

class Circle : public Shape {
public:
    void draw() override {
        cout << "Drawing a circle" << endl;
    }
};

class Rectangle : public Shape {
public:
    void draw() override {
        cout << "Drawing a rectangle" << endl;
    }
};

int main() {
    Shape* shape;
    Circle circle;
    Rectangle rectangle;

    shape = &circle;
    shape->draw();  // Output: Drawing a circle
```

```cpp
    shape = &rectangle;
    shape->draw();  // Output: Drawing a rectangle

    return 0;
}
```

In this example, Shape is an abstract class with a pure virtual function draw(). The Circle and Rectangle classes override the draw() function. The abstract class Shape cannot be instantiated, but pointers to it can be used to call the appropriate derived class implementations at run-time.

5.4 Virtual Destructors

In C++, when you delete an object through a pointer to a base class, the destructor of the base class should be **virtual**. This ensures that the destructors of derived classes are called properly, avoiding memory leaks or undefined behavior.

Example:

cpp

```cpp
#include <iostream>
using namespace std;

class Base {
public:
   Base() {
      cout << "Base constructor called" << endl;
   }

   virtual ~Base() {
      cout << "Base destructor called" << endl;
   }
};

class Derived : public Base {
public:
   Derived() {
      cout << "Derived constructor called" << endl;
   }

   ~Derived() {
      cout << "Derived destructor called" << endl;
   }
};
```

```cpp
int main() {
    Base* basePtr = new Derived();
    delete basePtr;  // Properly calls both Base and Derived destructors
    return 0;
}
```

The output will be:

```sql
Base constructor called
Derived constructor called
Derived destructor called
Base destructor called
```

Without the virtual destructor in the Base class, the Derived class destructor would not be called, potentially leading to memory leaks.

5.5 Benefits of Polymorphism

Polymorphism in C++ offers several key benefits:

Code Reusability: With polymorphism, you can write generic functions and classes that work with different types.

Flexibility: Run-time polymorphism allows you to add new functionality to a program without altering existing code, as long as it adheres to the base class interface.

Simplified Code Maintenance: Polymorphism promotes clean and modular code, making it easier to maintain and extend.

Abstraction: Through the use of abstract classes and interfaces, polymorphism enables high levels of abstraction in system design.

Conclusion

Polymorphism is one of the most powerful and flexible features of object-oriented programming in C++. By leveraging both compile-time polymorphism (through function and operator overloading) and run-time polymorphism (through virtual functions and pointers), you can write more maintainable, scalable, and reusable code. Polymorphism also helps to adhere to key design principles like **open/closed principle**, allowing systems to be extended with new behavior without modifying existing code.

In the next chapter, we will delve into **Encapsulation and Data Hiding**, two other important aspects of OOP that help in organizing and protecting the data within your C++ programs.

Chapter 6: Encapsulation and Data Hiding in C++

Encapsulation is a core concept in object-oriented programming (OOP) that refers to bundling the data (attributes) and methods (functions) that operate on the data into a single unit or class. It also involves restricting direct access to certain components of an object, which is referred to as **data hiding**. Encapsulation allows you to enforce control over how data is accessed and modified, ensuring that the internal state of an object is maintained in a valid, consistent manner.

In this chapter, we will explore the principles of encapsulation and data hiding in C++, discuss the advantages they provide, and examine real-world examples of how to implement and leverage these concepts.

6.1 What is Encapsulation?

Encapsulation is the practice of keeping the data (member variables) and the functions (member methods) that manipulate the data together in a class. This allows the class to be treated as a black box, where the internal workings are hidden from the outside world, and access is controlled through public methods.

In C++, encapsulation is achieved by defining classes with specific **access specifiers** that control the visibility of the class members.

Example of Encapsulation:

cpp

```cpp
#include <iostream>
using namespace std;

class Employee {
private:
    string name;
    int age;
    double salary;

public:
    // Constructor
```

```cpp
    Employee(string empName, int empAge, double empSalary) {
        name = empName;
        age = empAge;
        salary = empSalary;
    }

    // Public method to display employee details
    void displayInfo() {
        cout << "Name: " << name << endl;
        cout << "Age: " << age << endl;
        cout << "Salary: $" << salary << endl;
    }

    // Method to update salary
    void updateSalary(double newSalary) {
        if (newSalary > 0) {
            salary = newSalary;
        } else {
            cout << "Invalid salary!" << endl;
        }
    }
};

int main() {
    Employee emp1("Alice", 30, 60000);
```

```cpp
    emp1.displayInfo();  // Accessing data via public method

    emp1.updateSalary(65000);  // Updating salary
    emp1.displayInfo();        // Updated info
    return 0;
}
```

In the above example, the class Employee encapsulates the data members (name, age, and salary) and the member functions (displayInfo() and updateSalary()), which operate on that data. The private keyword ensures that the attributes are not accessible directly from outside the class. Instead, the class provides public methods that manage access and enforce validation, such as ensuring that salary updates are positive.

6.2 Data Hiding

Data hiding refers to the principle of restricting direct access to certain attributes and methods of an object to protect its internal state. By using **private** and **protected** access specifiers, C++

allows you to control which parts of an object are exposed to other parts of the program.

This not only enforces **data integrity** by preventing unintended or unauthorized changes but also encourages users to interact with objects only through well-defined interfaces (public methods), making the class easier to maintain and extend.

Example of Data Hiding:

cpp

```cpp
#include <iostream>
using namespace std;

class BankAccount {
private:
    double balance;  // Hidden from outside access

public:
    BankAccount(double initialBalance) {
        if (initialBalance > 0) {
            balance = initialBalance;
        } else {
            balance = 0;
```

        }
    }

    // Public method to deposit money
    void deposit(double amount) {
        if (amount > 0) {
            balance += amount;
        } else {
            cout << "Invalid deposit amount!" << endl;
        }
    }

    // Public method to withdraw money
    void withdraw(double amount) {
        if (amount > 0 && amount <= balance) {
            balance -= amount;
        } else {
            cout << "Invalid withdrawal amount!" << endl;
        }
    }

    // Public method to check balance
    double getBalance() const {
        return balance;
    }

};

```cpp
int main() {
    BankAccount account(1000);  // Initial balance of $1000
    account.deposit(500);      // Deposit $500
    cout << "Balance: $" << account.getBalance() << endl;

    account.withdraw(300);     // Withdraw $300
    cout << "Balance: $" << account.getBalance() << endl;

    return 0;
}
```

Here, the balance of the BankAccount class is **hidden** from direct access by declaring it as private. Instead, we provide public methods like deposit(), withdraw(), and getBalance() to interact with the balance in a controlled manner.

6.3 Access Specifiers in C++

C++ provides three key access specifiers that allow you to control the visibility of class members:

Private:

Members declared as `private` are not accessible outside the class.

Only the class's own methods can access and modify private members.

Public:

Members declared as `public` are accessible from outside the class.

This is typically used for methods that allow interaction with private data.

Protected:

Members declared as `protected` are similar to private members but are also accessible to derived classes.

This is useful in inheritance, as derived classes can access protected members of the base class.

Example of Access Specifiers:

cpp

```cpp
#include <iostream>
using namespace std;

class Base {
private:
    int privateVar;  // Only accessible within the Base class

protected:
    int protectedVar;  // Accessible to derived classes

public:
    int publicVar;  // Accessible from anywhere

    Base() : privateVar(1), protectedVar(2), publicVar(3) {}
};

class Derived : public Base {
public:
    void display() {
        // Cannot access privateVar directly
```

```cpp
    // cout << privateVar << endl;   // This will cause a compilation error

    // Can access protectedVar and publicVar
    cout << "Protected var: " << protectedVar << endl;
    cout << "Public var: " << publicVar << endl;
  }
};

int main() {
  Derived obj;
  obj.display();

  // Can access publicVar directly, but not protectedVar or privateVar
  cout << "Public var (main): " << obj.publicVar << endl;
  return 0;
}
```

In the example above, the derived class Derived can access protectedVar from the base class Base but cannot access privateVar. The public member publicVar is accessible to everyone.

6.4 Getters and Setters

To maintain the encapsulation and data hiding principles, C++ uses **getters** (also known as accessors) and **setters** (also known as mutators) to control access to private attributes. Getters retrieve the value of a private member, while setters allow controlled modification of private members, often including validation checks.

Example of Getters and Setters:

cpp

```cpp
#include <iostream>
using namespace std;

class Person {
private:
    string name;
    int age;

public:
    // Setter for name
    void setName(string newName) {
        if (!newName.empty()) {
```

```cpp
            name = newName;
        }
    }

    // Getter for name
    string getName() const {
        return name;
    }

    // Setter for age
    void setAge(int newAge) {
        if (newAge > 0) {
            age = newAge;
        }
    }

    // Getter for age
    int getAge() const {
        return age;
    }
};

int main() {
    Person person;
    person.setName("John Doe");
    person.setAge(25);
```

```cpp
cout << "Name: " << person.getName() << endl;
cout << "Age: " << person.getAge() << endl;

return 0;
}
```

In the above example, the private members name and age are modified only through setter methods, which include validation. The getter methods allow controlled access to retrieve the values of name and age.

6.5 Advantages of Encapsulation and Data Hiding

Encapsulation and data hiding offer several benefits:

Data Protection: By hiding internal details, encapsulation protects the data from unauthorized or unintended access and modifications.

Data Integrity: With controlled access through getters and setters, you can ensure that only valid data is stored, thereby maintaining data integrity.

Modular Design: Encapsulation promotes a modular approach to software design. Each class is responsible for managing its own data and behavior, which makes the code more maintainable.

Ease of Maintenance: Since the internal workings of a class are hidden, changes can be made to the class's implementation without affecting other parts of the program that use the class.

Flexibility and Reusability: Encapsulation allows for better code reuse by encapsulating functionality within self-contained objects that can be used across different parts of the application.

6.6 Real-World Example: Encapsulation in Software Design

Consider a banking application where you need to manage customer data, such as account balance and transaction history. By encapsulating the data in a BankAccount class, you can protect sensitive information and only allow valid operations through well-defined methods.

Chapter 7: Inheritance in C++

Inheritance is a fundamental feature of object-oriented programming (OOP) that allows a new class to inherit properties and behaviors (attributes and methods) from an existing class. This mechanism promotes code reusability and establishes a hierarchical relationship between classes. In C++, inheritance enables you to create a base class (also known as a parent or superclass) and one or more derived classes (children or subclasses) that extend or customize the functionality of the base class.

In this chapter, we will explore the various aspects of inheritance in C++, including its types, syntax, benefits, and practical examples.

7.1 What is Inheritance?

Inheritance allows a derived class to inherit the characteristics of a base class. The derived class can access and modify the properties and methods of the base class, as well as add new members specific to its implementation. This promotes code reuse, as common functionality can be defined in a base class and shared across multiple derived classes.

The general syntax for inheritance in C++ is:

cpp

```
class    DerivedClassName   :    access_specifier BaseClassName {
    // Members of derived class
};
```

Access Specifiers:

public: Members of the base class become public members of the derived class.

protected: Members of the base class become protected members of the derived class.

private: Members of the base class become private members of the derived class.

7.2 Types of Inheritance

C++ supports several types of inheritance, including:

Single Inheritance: A derived class inherits from a single base class.

Multiple Inheritance: A derived class inherits from multiple base classes.

Multilevel Inheritance: A derived class is derived from another derived class.

Hierarchical Inheritance: Multiple derived classes inherit from a single base class.

Hybrid Inheritance: A combination of two or more types of inheritance.

7.2.1 Single Inheritance

In single inheritance, a derived class inherits from one base class.

Example:

cpp

```cpp
#include <iostream>
using namespace std;

class Animal {
public:
    void eat() {
        cout << "Eating..." << endl;
    }
};

class Dog : public Animal {
public:
    void bark() {
        cout << "Barking..." << endl;
    }
};

int main() {
    Dog myDog;
    myDog.eat();  // Inherited method
    myDog.bark(); // Dog's own method
    return 0;
}
```

In this example, the Dog class inherits from the Animal class, allowing it to access the eat() method.

7.2.2 Multiple Inheritance

In multiple inheritance, a derived class can inherit from more than one base class.

Example:

cpp

```
#include <iostream>
using namespace std;

class Flyer {
public:
   void fly() {
      cout << "Flying..." << endl;
   }
};

class Swimmer {
public:
   void swim() {
      cout << "Swimming..." << endl;
```

    }
};

class Duck : public Flyer, public Swimmer {
public:
    void quack() {
        cout << "Quacking..." << endl;
    }
};

int main() {
    Duck myDuck;
    myDuck.fly(); // Method from Flyer
    myDuck.swim(); // Method from Swimmer
    myDuck.quack(); // Duck's own method
    return 0;
}
```

In this example, the Duck class inherits from both Flyer and Swimmer, gaining the ability to perform both actions.

### 7.2.3 Multilevel Inheritance

In multilevel inheritance, a class is derived from another derived class.
```

Example:

cpp

```cpp
#include <iostream>
using namespace std;

class Animal {
public:
    void eat() {
        cout << "Eating..." << endl;
    }
};

class Dog : public Animal {
public:
    void bark() {
        cout << "Barking..." << endl;
    }
};

class Puppy : public Dog {
public:
    void weep() {
        cout << "Weeping..." << endl;
    }
```

};

```cpp
int main() {
    Puppy myPuppy;
    myPuppy.eat();  // Inherited from Animal
    myPuppy.bark(); // Inherited from Dog
    myPuppy.weep(); // Puppy's own method
    return 0;
}
```

Here, Puppy inherits from Dog, which in turn inherits from Animal, forming a multilevel hierarchy.

7.2.4 Hierarchical Inheritance

In hierarchical inheritance, multiple derived classes inherit from a single base class.

Example:

cpp

```cpp
#include <iostream>
using namespace std;
```

```cpp
class Animal {
public:
   void eat() {
      cout << "Eating..." << endl;
   }
};

class Dog : public Animal {
public:
   void bark() {
      cout << "Barking..." << endl;
   }
};

class Cat : public Animal {
public:
   void meow() {
      cout << "Meowing..." << endl;
   }
};

int main() {
   Dog myDog;
   Cat myCat;

   myDog.eat(); // Method from Animal
```

```cpp
    myDog.bark(); // Dog's own method

    myCat.eat(); // Method from Animal
    myCat.meow(); // Cat's own method
    return 0;
}
```

Both Dog and Cat inherit from Animal, demonstrating hierarchical inheritance.

7.3 Virtual Inheritance

Virtual inheritance is a C++ feature that resolves the ambiguity arising from multiple inheritance. When two or more classes inherit from a common base class, a derived class can inherit that base class virtually to ensure that only one copy of the base class exists.

Example:

cpp

```cpp
#include <iostream>
using namespace std;
```

```cpp
class Base {
public:
    void show() {
        cout << "Base class show() function called." << endl;
    }
};

class Derived1 : virtual public Base {
};

class Derived2 : virtual public Base {
};

class Derived3 : public Derived1, public Derived2 {
};

int main() {
    Derived3 obj;
    obj.show(); // Calls show() from Base class, no ambiguity
    return 0;
}
```

In this example, both Derived1 and Derived2 inherit Base virtually, ensuring that only one instance of Base exists in Derived3.

7.4 Accessing Base Class Members

In derived classes, you can access public and protected members of the base class directly. However, private members cannot be accessed directly. To access private members, you can use protected or public member functions of the base class.

Example:

cpp

```cpp
#include <iostream>
using namespace std;

class Base {
private:
    int privateVar;

protected:
```

```cpp
    int protectedVar;

public:
    int publicVar;

    Base() : privateVar(1), protectedVar(2), publicVar(3) {}
};

class Derived : public Base {
public:
    void display() {
        // cout << privateVar; // Not accessible
        cout << "Protected var: " << protectedVar << endl; // Accessible
        cout << "Public var: " << publicVar << endl; // Accessible
    }
};

int main() {
    Derived obj;
    obj.display();
    // cout << obj.privateVar; // Not accessible
    return 0;
}
```

The derived class Derived can access the protected and public members of Base but not the private members.

7.5 Benefits of Inheritance

Inheritance provides several advantages, including:

Code Reusability: Common functionality can be defined in a base class and reused across derived classes, reducing code duplication.

Hierarchical Classification: Inheritance models real-world relationships more accurately, enabling a logical hierarchy.

Extensibility: You can extend the functionality of existing classes by creating new derived classes, facilitating easier updates and maintenance.

Polymorphism: Inheritance supports polymorphism, allowing for dynamic method binding and interface consistency.

Reduced Complexity: By breaking down complex systems into a hierarchy of classes, inheritance can simplify code structure and maintenance.

7.6 Real-World Example: Inheritance in Software Design

Consider a software system for managing different types of vehicles. You could create a base class Vehicle that contains common attributes like make, model, and methods like start() and stop(). Then, you could derive classes such as Car, Truck, and Motorcycle from the Vehicle class, adding specific attributes and methods relevant to each vehicle type.

Example:

cpp

```cpp
#include <iostream>
using namespace std;

class Vehicle {
```

```cpp
public:
    string make;
    string model;

    Vehicle(string m, string mod) : make(m), model(mod) {}

    void start() {
        cout << "Starting " << make << " " << model << endl;
    }

    void stop() {
        cout << "Stopping " << make << " " << model << endl;
    }
};

class Car : public Vehicle {
public:
    int numDoors;

    Car(string m, string mod, int doors) : Vehicle(m, mod), numDoors(doors) {}

    void displayInfo() {
```

```cpp
        cout << "Car Make: " << make << ", Model: " << model << ", Doors: " << numDoors << endl;
    }
};

class Truck : public Vehicle {
public:
    double loadCapacity;

    Truck(string m, string mod, double capacity) : Vehicle(m, mod), loadCapacity(capacity) {}

    void displayInfo() {
        cout << "Truck Make: " << make << ", Model: " << model << ", Load Capacity: " << loadCapacity << " tons" << endl;
    }
};

int main() {
    Car myCar("Toyota", "Camry", 4);
    myCar.start(); // Inherited method
    myCar.displayInfo(); // Car-specific method
    myCar.stop(); // Inherited method

    Truck myTruck("Ford", "F-150", 3.5);
```

```cpp
    myTruck.start(); // Inherited method
    myTruck.displayInfo(); // Truck-specific method
    myTruck.stop(); // Inherited method

    return 0;
}
```

In this example, we have a Vehicle class as the base class and two derived classes: Car and Truck. Each derived class has its specific attributes and methods but also inherits common functionality from the Vehicle class. This design illustrates how inheritance promotes code reuse and modular design.

7.7 Summary

In this chapter, we explored the concept of inheritance in C++. We discussed the different types of inheritance, including single, multiple, multilevel, hierarchical, and hybrid inheritance. We also covered the importance of virtual inheritance to avoid ambiguity in multiple inheritance scenarios.

Key points included:

Encapsulation of Common Functionality: Inheritance allows a derived class to reuse code from a base class, simplifying code maintenance.

Access Control: Understanding how public, protected, and private access specifiers affect member accessibility in derived classes.

Real-World Applications: Utilizing inheritance to create logical hierarchies in software design, such as vehicle management systems, showcases the practical benefits of inheritance.

Inheritance is a powerful feature in C++ that enables developers to create robust, maintainable, and scalable applications by leveraging existing code and relationships among classes.

Chapter 8: Polymorphism in C++

Polymorphism is one of the core concepts of object-oriented programming (OOP), allowing objects of different classes to be treated as objects of a common base class. It enables a single interface to represent different underlying forms (data types). In C++, polymorphism is typically achieved through function overloading, operator overloading, and virtual functions.

In this chapter, we will delve into the different types of polymorphism in C++, how to implement them, and their practical applications.

8.1 What is Polymorphism?

The term "polymorphism" means "many forms." In programming, it refers to the ability of different classes to be treated as instances of the same class through a common interface. There are two main types of polymorphism:

Compile-Time Polymorphism: Achieved through function overloading and operator overloading. This type of polymorphism is resolved during compile time.

Run-Time Polymorphism: Achieved through method overriding using virtual functions. This type of polymorphism is resolved during run time.

8.2 Compile-Time Polymorphism

Compile-time polymorphism is implemented through function overloading and operator overloading.

8.2.1 Function Overloading

Function overloading allows multiple functions to have the same name with different parameters (type or number). The compiler determines which function to call based on the arguments passed.

Example:

```cpp
#include <iostream>
using namespace std;

class Math {
public:
    // Function to add two integers
    int add(int a, int b) {
        return a + b;
    }

    // Function to add three integers
    int add(int a, int b, int c) {
        return a + b + c;
    }

    // Function to add two double values
    double add(double a, double b) {
        return a + b;
    }
};

int main() {
    Math math;
```

```cpp
    cout << "Sum of 3 and 4: " << math.add(3, 4) << endl; // Calls the first add
    cout << "Sum of 3, 4, and 5: " << math.add(3, 4, 5) << endl; // Calls the second add
    cout << "Sum of 3.5 and 2.5: " << math.add(3.5, 2.5) << endl; // Calls the third add
    return 0;
}
```

In this example, the add function is overloaded with different parameters, demonstrating compile-time polymorphism.

8.2.2 Operator Overloading

Operator overloading allows you to define custom behavior for operators (like +, -, *, etc.) when they are applied to objects of user-defined classes.

Example:

cpp

```cpp
#include <iostream>
using namespace std;
```

```cpp
class Complex {
public:
    float real;
    float imag;

    Complex(float r = 0, float i = 0) : real(r), imag(i)
{}

    // Overloading the + operator
    Complex operator+(const Complex& other) {
        return Complex(real + other.real, imag + other.imag);
    }

    void display() {
        cout << real << " + " << imag << "i" << endl;
    }
};

int main() {
    Complex c1(3.5, 2.5);
    Complex c2(1.5, 4.5);
    Complex c3 = c1 + c2; // Uses overloaded +
    c3.display(); // Output: 5 + 7i
    return 0;
```

}

In this example, the + operator is overloaded for the Complex class, allowing two complex numbers to be added together.

8.3 Run-Time Polymorphism

Run-time polymorphism is achieved through inheritance and virtual functions, allowing you to call derived class methods using base class pointers or references.

8.3.1 Virtual Functions

A virtual function is a member function that is declared in the base class and is overridden in a derived class. The keyword virtual is used in the base class to indicate that the function can be overridden.

Example:

cpp

```cpp
#include <iostream>
using namespace std;

class Base {
public:
    virtual void show() {
        cout << "Base class show() function called." << endl;
    }
};

class Derived : public Base {
public:
    void show() override {
        cout << "Derived class show() function called." << endl;
    }
};

void display(Base* b) {
    b->show();  // Calls the appropriate show() function
}

int main() {
    Base b;
```

```
Derived d;

display(&b); // Calls Base's show()
display(&d); // Calls Derived's show()
return 0;
}
```

In this example, the show function is declared as virtual in the Base class. When called through a base class pointer, it dynamically binds to the correct function based on the actual object type.

8.4 Advantages of Polymorphism

Code Flexibility: Polymorphism allows you to write more generic code. You can work with base class references or pointers, enabling you to pass different derived class objects to functions.

Enhanced Maintainability: Code changes or extensions are easier since you can introduce new derived classes without modifying existing code.

Dynamic Binding: It provides the ability to make decisions at runtime based on the object being pointed to, making your applications more flexible and dynamic.

8.5 Real-World Example: Polymorphism in Software Design

Consider a graphics application that can handle different shapes like circles, rectangles, and triangles. You can create a base class Shape and derive classes for each specific shape. Using polymorphism, you can manage these shapes using a single interface.

Example:

cpp

```
#include <iostream>
#include <vector>
using namespace std;

class Shape {
public:
```

```cpp
    virtual void draw() = 0; // Pure virtual function
};

class Circle : public Shape {
public:
    void draw() override {
        cout << "Drawing Circle" << endl;
    }
};

class Rectangle : public Shape {
public:
    void draw() override {
        cout << "Drawing Rectangle" << endl;
    }
};

class Triangle : public Shape {
public:
    void draw() override {
        cout << "Drawing Triangle" << endl;
    }
};

int main() {
    vector<Shape*> shapes;
```

```cpp
    shapes.push_back(new Circle());
    shapes.push_back(new Rectangle());
    shapes.push_back(new Triangle());

    for (Shape* shape : shapes) {
        shape->draw(); // Calls the appropriate draw() method
    }

    // Clean up
    for (Shape* shape : shapes) {
        delete shape;
    }

    return 0;
}
```

In this example, we create a base class Shape with a pure virtual function draw(). The derived classes Circle, Rectangle, and Triangle implement their specific draw() methods. A vector of Shape pointers allows us to manage and draw different shapes using a unified interface, showcasing the power of polymorphism.

8.6 Summary

In this chapter, we covered the concept of polymorphism in C++. We explored:

Compile-Time Polymorphism: Achieved through function overloading and operator overloading, allowing functions and operators to have multiple forms based on input types.

Run-Time Polymorphism: Achieved through virtual functions and inheritance, allowing method overriding and dynamic binding based on the actual object type at runtime.

Advantages of Polymorphism: Enhanced code flexibility, maintainability, and dynamic behavior in applications.

Polymorphism is a crucial concept in C++ that allows developers to create flexible, reusable, and scalable code, facilitating the design of robust applications.

Chapter 9: Abstract Classes and Interfaces in C++

Abstract classes and interfaces are key components of object-oriented programming in C++. They allow you to define a contract for derived classes, specifying methods that must be implemented while providing a way to enforce certain behaviors across different classes. This chapter will cover the concepts of abstract classes, interfaces, their syntax, usage, and real-world applications in C++.

9.1 What is an Abstract Class?

An abstract class is a class that cannot be instantiated on its own and is intended to be a base class for other derived classes. It may contain pure virtual functions, which are functions that have no implementation in the base class and must be overridden in any derived class.

To declare a pure virtual function, you use the = 0 syntax in the class definition.

Example:

cpp

```cpp
#include <iostream>
using namespace std;

class AbstractShape {
public:
    virtual void draw() = 0; // Pure virtual function
};

class Circle : public AbstractShape {
public:
    void draw() override {
        cout << "Drawing Circle" << endl;
    }
};

class Square : public AbstractShape {
public:
    void draw() override {
        cout << "Drawing Square" << endl;
```

    }
};

In this example, `AbstractShape` is an abstract class with a pure virtual function `draw()`. The derived classes `Circle` and `Square` provide their implementations of the `draw()` method.

9.2 Defining an Abstract Class

To define an abstract class in C++, follow these steps:

Use the `class` keyword to declare the class.

Declare one or more pure virtual functions using the `= 0` syntax.

Optionally, you can provide implementations for some non-pure virtual functions or regular member functions.

Example:

cpp

```cpp
class Vehicle {
public:
    virtual void start() = 0; // Pure virtual function
    virtual void stop() {
        cout << "Vehicle stopped." << endl; // Concrete implementation
    }
};
```

In this example, Vehicle is an abstract class with a pure virtual function start(), and a concrete method stop() that can be inherited by derived classes.

9.3 Interfaces in C++

While C++ does not have a specific keyword for interfaces like some other programming languages (e.g., Java), you can achieve interface-like behavior using abstract classes. An interface in C++ is typically defined as an abstract class that contains only pure virtual functions.

Example:

cpp

```cpp
class Drawable {
public:
    virtual void draw() = 0; // Pure virtual function
    virtual void resize() = 0; // Another pure virtual function
};

class Rectangle : public Drawable {
public:
    void draw() override {
        cout << "Drawing Rectangle" << endl;
    }

    void resize() override {
        cout << "Resizing Rectangle" << endl;
    }
};
```

In this example, Drawable acts as an interface, and Rectangle implements the methods defined in the interface.

9.4 Benefits of Abstract Classes and Interfaces

Code Consistency: Abstract classes and interfaces enforce a consistent API across different derived classes, ensuring that all implementing classes adhere to the same contract.

Decoupling: They promote loose coupling between classes, allowing changes to one class without affecting others as long as the interface remains unchanged.

Reusability: Common functionality can be implemented in base classes while derived classes focus on specific behavior, promoting code reuse.

Enhanced Design: They provide a clear structure and guidelines for class design, making the codebase easier to understand and maintain.

9.5 Real-World Example: Abstract Classes and Interfaces in Software Design

Consider a payment processing system where various payment methods (like Credit Card, PayPal, and Bitcoin) implement a common interface for processing payments. You can create an abstract class PaymentMethod with a pure virtual function processPayment().

Example:

cpp

```
#include <iostream>
using namespace std;

class PaymentMethod {
public:
    virtual void processPayment(double amount) = 0;  // Pure virtual function
};

class CreditCard : public PaymentMethod {
public:
    void processPayment(double amount) override {
        cout << "Processing credit card payment of $" << amount << endl;
    }
```

};

```cpp
class PayPal : public PaymentMethod {
public:
    void processPayment(double amount) override {
        cout << "Processing PayPal payment of $" << amount << endl;
    }
};

class Bitcoin : public PaymentMethod {
public:
    void processPayment(double amount) override {
        cout << "Processing Bitcoin payment of $" << amount << endl;
    }
};

int main() {
    PaymentMethod* payment1 = new CreditCard();
    PaymentMethod* payment2 = new PayPal();
    PaymentMethod* payment3 = new Bitcoin();

    payment1->processPayment(150.0);   // Calls CreditCard's method
```

```
    payment2->processPayment(200.0);    // Calls PayPal's method
    payment3->processPayment(0.05);     // Calls Bitcoin's method

    // Clean up
    delete payment1;
    delete payment2;
    delete payment3;

    return 0;
}
```

In this example, PaymentMethod serves as an abstract class with a pure virtual function processPayment(). **The derived classes (**CreditCard, PayPal, Bitcoin**) implement this function, providing specific payment processing behavior. This design allows you to manage different payment methods uniformly through the base class pointer.**

9.6 Summary

In this chapter, we discussed:

Abstract Classes: Classes that cannot be instantiated and contain pure virtual functions that must be implemented by derived classes.

Interfaces: Achieved in C++ using abstract classes that define a contract through pure virtual functions.

Benefits: Enforcing consistency, promoting code reusability, and decoupling class implementations for easier maintenance and scalability.

Abstract classes and interfaces are vital for designing robust, maintainable systems in C++. They provide a structured approach to defining behaviors and ensure that different classes adhere to a common set of functionalities, enhancing code quality and flexibility.

Chapter 10: Exception Handling in C++

Exception handling is a critical aspect of robust software development, allowing programs to manage errors gracefully and maintain stability during runtime. C++ provides a powerful mechanism for handling exceptions, enabling developers to write cleaner, more reliable code. In this chapter, we will explore the concepts of exception handling, the syntax used in C++, and best practices for implementing exception handling in your applications.

10.1 Understanding Exceptions

An exception is an unexpected event that occurs during the execution of a program, disrupting the normal flow of instructions. Common exceptions include runtime errors like division by zero, accessing invalid memory, and file I/O errors.

When an exception is thrown, control is transferred to a predefined exception handler, which can take appropriate actions to resolve the issue or log it for later analysis.

10.2 Basic Syntax of Exception Handling in C++

C++ provides three primary keywords for exception handling: try, catch, and throw.

try block: This block contains code that may throw an exception.

catch block: This block defines how to handle specific exceptions thrown by the try block.

throw statement: This statement is used to throw an exception when an error occurs.

Example:

cpp

```
#include <iostream>
using namespace std;

void divide(int a, int b) {
    if (b == 0) {
```

```cpp
        throw runtime_error("Division by zero error"); // Throwing an exception
    }
    cout << "Result: " << a / b << endl;
}

int main() {
    try {
        divide(10, 0); // This will throw an exception
    } catch (const runtime_error& e) {
        cout << "Caught an exception: " << e.what() << endl; // Handling the exception
    }
    return 0;
}
```

In this example, the `divide` function throws a `runtime_error` exception if an attempt is made to divide by zero. The `main` function contains a `try` block that calls `divide`, and a `catch` block to handle the exception.

10.3 Multiple Exceptions

You can have multiple catch blocks to handle different types of exceptions thrown by a try block. The catch blocks should be ordered from most specific to most general.

Example:

cpp

```cpp
#include <iostream>
using namespace std;

void process(int value) {
    if (value < 0) {
        throw invalid_argument("Negative value error");
    } else if (value == 0) {
        throw runtime_error("Zero value error");
    }
    cout << "Processing value: " << value << endl;
}

int main() {
    try {
        process(-5); // Throws invalid_argument
    } catch (const invalid_argument& e) {
```

```
      cout << "Caught an exception: " << e.what() << endl;
   } catch (const runtime_error& e) {
      cout << "Caught an exception: " << e.what() << endl;
   }
   return 0;
}
```

In this example, the process function throws different exceptions based on the input value. The main function has separate catch blocks to handle each specific exception type.

10.4 Catching All Exceptions

You can catch all exceptions using an ellipsis ... in the catch block. This is useful for handling unexpected exceptions.

Example:

cpp

#include <iostream>

```cpp
using namespace std;

void riskyFunction() {
    throw "Something went wrong"; // Throwing a string exception
}

int main() {
    try {
        riskyFunction();
    } catch (...) {
        cout << "Caught an unknown exception." << endl; // Catching all exceptions
    }
    return 0;
}
```

In this example, the catch block with ... captures any type of exception, providing a fallback mechanism for error handling.

10.5 Creating Custom Exceptions

You can create custom exception classes by inheriting from the standard exception classes. This allows you to define specific error conditions in your applications.

Example:

cpp

```
#include <iostream>
#include <exception>
using namespace std;

class CustomException : public exception {
public:
    const char* what() const noexcept override {
        return "This is a custom exception";
    }
};

void triggerException() {
    throw CustomException(); // Throwing a custom exception
}

int main() {
```

```
    try {
        triggerException();
    } catch (const CustomException& e) {
        cout << "Caught a custom exception: " << e.what() << endl; // Handling custom exception
    }
    return 0;
}
```

In this example, CustomException is a user-defined exception class that overrides the what() method to provide a custom error message. This custom exception can be thrown and caught just like standard exceptions.

10.6 Best Practices for Exception Handling

Use Exceptions for Exceptional Cases: Exceptions should be reserved for unexpected situations. Do not use exceptions for regular control flow.

Catch by Reference: Catch exceptions by reference to avoid slicing and unnecessary copies. Use const reference when possible.

Order of Catch Blocks: Always catch more specific exceptions before more general ones to ensure that the correct handler is invoked.

Resource Management: Use RAII (Resource Acquisition Is Initialization) to manage resources and ensure they are released even if an exception occurs. Smart pointers (e.g., std::unique_ptr, std::shared_ptr) can help manage memory automatically.

Logging and Cleanup: Log exception information and ensure that resources are cleaned up in case of an exception. You can use finally blocks in combination with RAII.

10.7 Summary

In this chapter, we discussed:

Exceptions: Unforeseen events that disrupt the normal flow of a program.

Exception Handling Syntax: The use of try, catch, and throw statements to manage exceptions.

Multiple Exceptions: Handling different types of exceptions using multiple catch blocks.

Custom Exceptions: Creating user-defined exception classes for more specific error handling.

Best Practices: Guidelines for effective exception handling, including the use of RAII and logging.

Exception handling is an essential feature in C++ that helps developers build resilient applications. By understanding and implementing effective exception handling strategies, you can ensure that your applications remain stable and maintainable even in the face of unexpected errors.

Chapter 11: Templates in C++: Generic Programming

Templates are a powerful feature of C++ that enables generic programming, allowing developers to write code that can work with any data type. This capability promotes code reuse and flexibility, as templates enable the creation of functions and classes that can operate on various types without sacrificing type safety. In this chapter, we will explore the different types of templates, their syntax, usage, and real-world applications in C++.

11.1 Understanding Templates

A template is a blueprint for creating functions or classes. Templates enable you to define a function or class that can operate on generic types, making your code more adaptable and reusable.

There are two primary types of templates in C++:

Function Templates: Allow you to create functions that can work with any data type.

Class Templates: Allow you to create classes that can handle any data type.

11.2 Function Templates

A function template is defined using the template keyword followed by template parameters. It allows you to create a single function that can operate on different types.

Syntax:

cpp

```
template <typename T>
T functionName(T param1, T param2) {
    // Function implementation
}
```

Example:

cpp

```cpp
#include <iostream>
using namespace std;

template <typename T>
T add(T a, T b) {
    return a + b;
}

int main() {
    cout << "Integer addition: " << add(3, 4) << endl; // Works with integers
    cout << "Double addition: " << add(3.5, 4.2) << endl; // Works with doubles
    return 0;
}
```

In this example, the `add` function template can add integers, doubles, or any other types that support the + operator.

11.3 Class Templates

Class templates allow you to define a class that can work with any data type. This is useful for creating generic data structures such as lists, stacks, or queues.

Syntax:

cpp

```
template <typename T>
class ClassName {
public:
    // Class members
};
```

Example:

cpp

```
#include <iostream>
using namespace std;

template <typename T>
class Pair {
private:
    T first;
```

```cpp
    T second;

public:
    Pair(T a, T b) : first(a), second(b) {}

    T getFirst() const { return first; }
    T getSecond() const { return second; }
};

int main() {
    Pair<int> intPair(1, 2);
    cout << "First: " << intPair.getFirst() << ", Second: " << intPair.getSecond() << endl;

    Pair<string> strPair("Hello", "World");
    cout << "First: " << strPair.getFirst() << ", Second: " << strPair.getSecond() << endl;

    return 0;
}
```

In this example, the `Pair` class template can store two values of the same type, demonstrating how templates enhance code reuse for different data types.

11.4 Template Specialization

Template specialization allows you to define specific implementations of a template for certain data types. This is useful when the default behavior of the template does not meet the requirements for specific types.

Example:

cpp

```
#include <iostream>
using namespace std;

template <typename T>
class Calculator {
public:
   static T add(T a, T b) {
      return a + b;
   }
};

// Template specialization for the `char` type
template <>
```

```cpp
class Calculator<char> {
public:
    static int add(char a, char b) {
        return a + b; // Returning the ASCII value sum
    }
};

int main() {
    cout << "Int addition: " << Calculator<int>::add(5, 10) << endl; // Uses generic implementation
    cout << "Char addition: " << Calculator<char>::add('A', 'B') << endl; // Uses specialized implementation
    return 0;
}
```

In this example, the Calculator class template has a specialized version for the char type, which adds their ASCII values instead of treating them as characters.

11.5 Variadic Templates

Variadic templates are a feature introduced in C++11 that allows you to create templates that accept a variable number of template parameters. This is particularly useful for functions that can take an arbitrary number of arguments.

Example:

cpp

```cpp
#include <iostream>
using namespace std;

template <typename T>
void print(T value) {
    cout << value << endl; // Base case for recursion
}

template <typename T, typename... Args>
void print(T first, Args... args) {
    cout << first << ", ";
    print(args...); // Recursive call with remaining arguments
}
```

```cpp
int main() {
    print(1, 2.5, "Hello", 'A'); // Can accept multiple types and numbers of arguments
    return 0;
}
```

In this example, the print function uses variadic templates to accept any number of arguments of various types, demonstrating the flexibility of templates.

11.6 Best Practices for Using Templates

Use Meaningful Names: Use descriptive names for template parameters to enhance code readability (e.g., typename T can be replaced with typename ItemType).

Limit Template Specialization: Only specialize templates when necessary. Excessive specialization can lead to code bloat and maintenance challenges.

Maintain Type Safety: Ensure that the operations in your template are valid for the types you expect to use. Use static_assert to enforce conditions at compile time.

Documentation: Document template usage and expected types, as templates can introduce complexity and may not be immediately clear to users.

Testing: Thoroughly test templates with various data types to ensure they behave correctly and handle edge cases.

11.7 Summary

In this chapter, we covered:

Templates: A powerful feature in C++ for generic programming, allowing code reuse and flexibility.

Function and Class Templates: How to define and use templates for functions and classes.

Template Specialization: Creating specific implementations of templates for certain data types.

Variadic Templates: Handling an arbitrary number of template parameters for functions.

Best Practices: Guidelines for using templates effectively in your C++ applications.

Templates are a cornerstone of modern C++ programming, enabling you to write efficient, reusable, and type-safe code. By mastering templates, you can create flexible applications that can easily adapt to various data types and use cases.

Chapter 12: Standard Template Library (STL) in C++

The Standard Template Library (STL) is a powerful set of C++ template classes that provide general-purpose classes and functions for handling data structures and algorithms. STL simplifies the implementation of common data structures and algorithms, promoting code reusability and efficiency. In this chapter, we will explore the components of the STL, including containers, iterators, algorithms, and more.

12.1 Overview of STL

STL is a collection of template classes that allow you to work with data in a generic way. It consists of four main components:

Containers: Data structures that store objects (e.g., vectors, lists, sets).

Iterators: Objects that provide a way to access elements in containers sequentially.

Algorithms: Functions that operate on containers and iterators to perform operations such as sorting, searching, and manipulating data.

Functors: Objects that can be called as if they were functions, often used with algorithms.

12.2 Containers

STL provides several types of containers, each designed for different use cases:

Vector: A dynamic array that can resize itself automatically when elements are added or removed.
Example:
cpp

```
#include <iostream>
#include <vector>
using namespace std;

int main() {
    vector<int> numbers = {1, 2, 3};
    numbers.push_back(4); // Adding an element
```

```cpp
    cout << "Vector size: " << numbers.size() << endl;

    for (int num : numbers) {
        cout << num << " "; // Accessing elements
    }
    cout << endl;
    return 0;
}
```

List: A doubly-linked list that allows efficient insertion and deletion of elements at any position.
Example:
cpp

```
#include <iostream>
#include <list>
using namespace std;

int main() {
    list<string> fruits = {"Apple", "Banana", "Cherry"};
    fruits.push_back("Orange"); // Adding to the end
```

```cpp
    fruits.push_front("Mango"); // Adding to the front

    for (const string& fruit : fruits) {
        cout << fruit << " "; // Accessing elements
    }
    cout << endl;
    return 0;
}
```

Set: A collection of unique elements stored in a specific order, typically used for fast retrieval.
Example:
cpp

```cpp
#include <iostream>
#include <set>
using namespace std;

int main() {
    set<int> uniqueNumbers = {3, 1, 2, 2}; // Duplicate will be ignored
    uniqueNumbers.insert(5);

    for (int num : uniqueNumbers) {
```

```cpp
        cout << num << " "; // Accessing unique elements
    }
    cout << endl;
    return 0;
}
```

Map: An associative container that stores key-value pairs, allowing fast retrieval based on keys.
Example:
cpp

```cpp
#include <iostream>
#include <map>
using namespace std;

int main() {
    map<string, int> ageMap;
    ageMap["Alice"] = 30;
    ageMap["Bob"] = 25;

    for (const auto& pair : ageMap) {
        cout << pair.first << ": " << pair.second << endl; // Accessing key-value pairs
```

    }
    return 0;
}

12.3 Iterators

Iterators provide a standardized way to traverse the elements in a container. They are similar to pointers and can be used to access and modify container elements.

Types of Iterators:

Input Iterator: Can read data from a container.

Output Iterator: Can write data to a container.

Forward Iterator: Can read/write data and move forward.

Bidirectional Iterator: Can move both forward and backward.

Random Access Iterator: Can move to any element in constant time.

Example:

cpp

```cpp
#include <iostream>
#include <vector>
using namespace std;

int main() {
    vector<int> numbers = {1, 2, 3, 4, 5};

    // Using an iterator to traverse the vector
    vector<int>::iterator it;
    for (it = numbers.begin(); it != numbers.end(); ++it) {
        cout << *it << " "; // Accessing elements
    }
    cout << endl;
    return 0;
}
```

12.4 Algorithms

STL provides a rich set of algorithms that can be used with containers. Common algorithms include sorting, searching, and manipulating data.

Sorting: Sort elements in a container using std::sort().
Example:
cpp

```
#include <iostream>
#include <vector>
#include <algorithm>
using namespace std;

int main() {
    vector<int> numbers = {5, 3, 1, 4, 2};
    sort(numbers.begin(), numbers.end()); // Sorting the vector

    for (int num : numbers) {
        cout << num << " "; // Accessing sorted elements
    }
    cout << endl;
    return 0;
}
```

Searching: Find an element in a container using std::find() or std::binary_search() for sorted ranges.

Example:

cpp

```cpp
#include <iostream>
#include <vector>
#include <algorithm>
using namespace std;

int main() {
    vector<int> numbers = {1, 2, 3, 4, 5};
    auto it = find(numbers.begin(), numbers.end(), 3); // Searching for 3

    if (it != numbers.end()) {
        cout << "Found: " << *it << endl; // Element found
    } else {
        cout << "Not Found" << endl; // Element not found
    }
    return 0;
}
```

Transforming: Use std::transform() to apply a function to a range of elements.
Example:
cpp
Copy code
```cpp
#include <iostream>
#include <vector>
#include <algorithm>
using namespace std;

int main() {
    vector<int> numbers = {1, 2, 3, 4, 5};
    vector<int> squares(numbers.size());

    transform(numbers.begin(), numbers.end(), squares.begin(), [](int x) {
        return x * x; // Squaring each element
    });

    for (int num : squares) {
        cout << num << " "; // Accessing transformed elements
    }
    cout << endl;
```

    return 0;
}

12.5 Functors

A functor is an object that can be called as if it were a function, typically by overloading the operator(). Functors are often used with algorithms to customize their behavior.

Example:

cpp

```
#include <iostream>
#include <vector>
#include <algorithm>
using namespace std;

class Square {
public:
    int operator()(int x) const {
        return x * x; // Functor to square a number
    }
```

};

```
int main() {
   vector<int> numbers = {1, 2, 3, 4, 5};
   vector<int> squares(numbers.size());

   transform(numbers.begin(), numbers.end(), squares.begin(), Square()); // Using functor

   for (int num : squares) {
      cout << num << " "; // Accessing squared numbers
   }
   cout << endl;
   return 0;
}
```

12.6 Best Practices for Using STL

Choose the Right Container: Select the appropriate container based on your needs (e.g., use a vector for dynamic arrays, a set for unique elements).

Use Algorithms: Leverage STL algorithms instead of writing your own for common tasks. They are often optimized and easier to read.

Avoid Unnecessary Copies: Use references or pointers when passing large containers to functions to avoid copying overhead.

Understand Iterators: Familiarize yourself with the different types of iterators and their use cases for efficient traversal of containers.

Stay Updated: STL continues to evolve with new features and improvements in newer C++ standards. Stay informed about updates in STL to take advantage of new functionalities.

12.7 Summary

In this chapter, we covered:

Standard Template Library (STL): A powerful set of template classes for data structures and algorithms.

Containers: Different types of containers, including vectors, lists, sets, and maps.

Iterators: The concept of iterators for traversing container elements.

Algorithms: A rich set of algorithms for common operations on containers.

Functors: Objects that can be called as functions, often used with algorithms.

Best Practices: Guidelines for effectively using STL in your applications.

The STL is an essential part of C++ programming, providing robust tools for managing data and implementing algorithms efficiently. By mastering the STL, you can write cleaner, more maintainable code that leverages the power of C++.

Chapter 13: Exception Handling in C++

Exception handling is a crucial aspect of modern C++ programming, allowing developers to manage errors and exceptional conditions gracefully. Proper use of exception handling improves the reliability and robustness of applications by preventing crashes and providing meaningful error messages. In this chapter, we will explore the concepts of exceptions, how to handle them in C++, and best practices for using exception handling effectively.

13.1 Understanding Exceptions

An exception is an event that occurs during the execution of a program that disrupts the normal flow of instructions. Common causes of exceptions include:

Division by zero

Accessing invalid memory

File I/O errors

Network issues

When an exception occurs, control is transferred to an appropriate exception handler, which can either resolve the issue or provide feedback to the user.

13.2 Exception Handling Basics

C++ provides a structured way to handle exceptions using three keywords: try, catch, and throw.

try: This block contains code that might throw an exception.

catch: This block handles the exception if it is thrown in the associated try block.

throw: This keyword is used to signal that an exception has occurred.

Syntax:

cpp

```cpp
try {
    // Code that may throw an exception
} catch (ExceptionType e) {
    // Code to handle the exception
}
```

Example:

cpp

```
#include <iostream>
using namespace std;

int divide(int a, int b) {
    if (b == 0) {
        throw runtime_error("Division by zero error!"); // Throwing an exception
    }
    return a / b;
}

int main() {
    try {
        cout << divide(10, 2) << endl; // Successful division
```

```cpp
    cout << divide(10, 0) << endl; // This will throw an exception
  } catch (const runtime_error& e) {
    cout << "Caught an exception: " << e.what() << endl; // Handling the exception
  }
  return 0;
}
```

In this example, the divide function throws a runtime_error when division by zero is attempted. The catch block handles the exception and prints an error message.

13.3 Multiple Catch Blocks

You can have multiple catch blocks to handle different types of exceptions. Each catch block can specify a different exception type.

Example:

cpp

```cpp
#include <iostream>
```

```cpp
#include <stdexcept>
using namespace std;

void test(int value) {
    if (value < 0) {
        throw invalid_argument("Negative value error!"); // Throws invalid_argument
    } else if (value == 0) {
        throw runtime_error("Zero value error!"); // Throws runtime_error
    }
}

int main() {
    try {
        test(-1);
    } catch (const invalid_argument& e) {
        cout << "Caught an exception: " << e.what() << endl; // Handling invalid_argument
    } catch (const runtime_error& e) {
        cout << "Caught an exception: " << e.what() << endl; // Handling runtime_error
    }
    return 0;
}
```

In this example, the `test` function can throw different types of exceptions based on the input value. Each `catch` block handles a specific exception type accordingly.

13.4 Catching All Exceptions

You can catch all exceptions using a catch-all handler, which uses an ellipsis (...). This is useful for logging or handling unexpected exceptions.

Example:

cpp

```cpp
#include <iostream>
using namespace std;

int main() {
    try {
        throw 42; // Throwing an integer exception
    } catch (...) { // Catching all exceptions
        cout << "Caught an unknown exception!" << endl;
    }
}
```

    return 0;
}

In this example, the catch-all handler catches any type of exception that is thrown.

13.5 Rethrowing Exceptions

Sometimes you may want to catch an exception and then rethrow it to allow further handling upstream. You can do this by simply using the throw; statement without specifying an exception.

Example:

cpp

```
#include <iostream>
#include <stdexcept>
using namespace std;

void process() {
    try {
        throw runtime_error("Something went wrong!"); // Throwing an exception
```

```cpp
    } catch (const runtime_error& e) {
        cout << "Caught: " << e.what() << endl; // Handling the exception
        throw; // Rethrowing the exception
    }
}

int main() {
    try {
        process();
    } catch (const runtime_error& e) {
        cout << "Rethrown exception: " << e.what() << endl; // Handling rethrown exception
    }
    return 0;
}
```

In this example, the exception thrown in the `process` function is caught, logged, and then rethrown to be handled in the `main` function.

13.6 Custom Exception Classes

You can create your own exception classes by inheriting from the standard exception classes. This allows you to define specific exceptions relevant to your application.

Example:

cpp

```cpp
#include <iostream>
#include <stdexcept>
using namespace std;

class MyException : public exception {
public:
    const char* what() const noexcept override {
        return "My custom exception occurred!";
    }
};

void test() {
    throw MyException();  // Throwing a custom exception
}

int main() {
```

```cpp
   try {
      test();
   } catch (const MyException& e) {
      cout << "Caught: " << e.what() << endl; // Handling custom exception
   }
   return 0;
}
```

In this example, MyException is a custom exception class that overrides the what() method to provide a specific error message.

13.7 Best Practices for Exception Handling

Use Exceptions for Exceptional Situations: Exceptions should be used for error handling in exceptional circumstances, not for regular control flow.

Catch by Reference: Catch exceptions by reference to avoid slicing and ensure the full exception object is preserved.

Limit Catch Blocks: Catch only those exceptions that you can handle appropriately, and avoid overly broad catch blocks unless necessary.

Provide Meaningful Messages: When throwing exceptions, provide meaningful messages to make debugging easier.

Clean Up Resources: Ensure that resources (e.g., memory, file handles) are released properly, even when exceptions are thrown. Use RAII (Resource Acquisition Is Initialization) principles where possible.

Document Exception Behavior: Clearly document the exceptions that can be thrown by functions, allowing users to handle them appropriately.

13.8 Summary

In this chapter, we covered:

Understanding Exceptions: What exceptions are and why they are important in C++.

Exception Handling Basics: The use of try, catch, and throw keywords for managing exceptions.

Multiple Catch Blocks: Handling different types of exceptions with multiple catch blocks.

Catching All Exceptions: Using catch-all handlers to catch unexpected exceptions.

Rethrowing Exceptions: How to rethrow exceptions for further handling.

Custom Exception Classes: Creating custom exception classes for specific error handling.

Best Practices: Guidelines for effective exception handling in C++.

Exception handling is a vital part of robust C++ programming, enabling developers to create resilient applications that can manage errors gracefully. By understanding and implementing effective exception handling strategies, you can significantly enhance the reliability of your applications.

Chapter 14: Design Patterns in C++

Design patterns are established solutions to common software design problems, providing a template for writing code that is efficient, reusable, and maintainable. In C++, design patterns can help developers tackle complex software architecture and design challenges effectively. In this chapter, we will explore various design patterns, categorize them, and provide real-world examples of how to implement these patterns in C++.

14.1 Understanding Design Patterns

Design patterns are classified into three main categories:

Creational Patterns: These patterns deal with object creation mechanisms, aiming to create objects in a manner suitable to the situation. Examples include Singleton, Factory, and Builder patterns.

Structural Patterns: These patterns focus on how objects are composed to form larger structures. Examples include Adapter, Composite, and Proxy patterns.

Behavioral Patterns: These patterns are concerned with the interactions and responsibilities of objects. Examples include Observer, Strategy, and Command patterns.

14.2 Creational Patterns

Singleton Pattern

The Singleton pattern ensures that a class has only one instance and provides a global access point to that instance. It is commonly used for managing shared resources like configuration settings.

Example:

cpp

```
#include <iostream>
using namespace std;

class Singleton {
```

```cpp
private:
    static Singleton* instance;

    // Private constructor to prevent instantiation
    Singleton() {}

public:
    static Singleton* getInstance() {
        if (!instance) {
            instance = new Singleton();
        }
        return instance;
    }

    void display() {
        cout << "Singleton Instance" << endl;
    }
};

Singleton* Singleton::instance = nullptr;

int main() {
    Singleton* s1 = Singleton::getInstance();
    Singleton* s2 = Singleton::getInstance();

    s1->display();
```

```
    cout << "Are both instances the same? " << (s1
== s2) << endl; // Output: 1 (true)
    return 0;
}
```

Factory Pattern

The Factory pattern provides an interface for creating objects but allows subclasses to alter the type of objects that will be created. This promotes loose coupling in the code.

Example:
cpp

```
#include <iostream>
using namespace std;

class Shape {
public:
    virtual void draw() = 0; // Pure virtual function
};

class Circle : public Shape {
public:
    void draw() override {
```

```cpp
        cout << "Drawing a Circle" << endl;
    }
};

class Square : public Shape {
public:
    void draw() override {
        cout << "Drawing a Square" << endl;
    }
};

class ShapeFactory {
public:
    static Shape* createShape(const string& shapeType) {
        if (shapeType == "Circle") {
            return new Circle();
        } else if (shapeType == "Square") {
            return new Square();
        }
        return nullptr;
    }
};

int main() {
```

```cpp
    Shape* shape1 = ShapeFactory::createShape("Circle");
    shape1->draw();

    Shape* shape2 = ShapeFactory::createShape("Square");
    shape2->draw();

    delete shape1;
    delete shape2;
    return 0;
}
```

14.3 Structural Patterns

Adapter Pattern

The Adapter pattern allows incompatible interfaces to work together by creating a wrapper around an existing class. This is useful when integrating new features into legacy systems.

Example:

cpp

```cpp
#include <iostream>
using namespace std;

class EuropeanSocket {
public:
   void connect() {
      cout << "European Socket Connected" << endl;
   }
};

class AmericanSocket {
public:
   void connect() {
      cout << "American Socket Connected" << endl;
   }
};

class SocketAdapter {
private:
   EuropeanSocket* europeanSocket;

public:
   SocketAdapter(EuropeanSocket* socket) : europeanSocket(socket) {}
```

```cpp
    void connect() {
        europeanSocket->connect();   // Adapting European socket
    }
};

int main() {
    EuropeanSocket* euroSocket = new EuropeanSocket();
    SocketAdapter* adapter = new SocketAdapter(euroSocket);
    adapter->connect(); // Using adapter to connect European socket

    delete euroSocket;
    delete adapter;
    return 0;
}
```

Composite Pattern

The Composite pattern allows you to compose objects into tree structures to represent part-whole hierarchies. This pattern enables clients to treat individual objects and compositions uniformly.

Example:

cpp

```cpp
#include <iostream>
#include <vector>
using namespace std;

class Component {
public:
    virtual void operation() = 0;
};

class Leaf : public Component {
public:
    void operation() override {
        cout << "Leaf Operation" << endl;
    }
};

class Composite : public Component {
private:
    vector<Component*> children;

public:
```

```cpp
    void add(Component* component) {
        children.push_back(component);
    }

    void operation() override {
        cout << "Composite Operation" << endl;
        for (Component* child : children) {
            child->operation(); // Delegating operation to children
        }
    }
};

int main() {
    Composite* root = new Composite();
    Leaf* leaf1 = new Leaf();
    Leaf* leaf2 = new Leaf();

    root->add(leaf1);
    root->add(leaf2);

    root->operation(); // Performing operation on composite

    delete leaf1;
    delete leaf2;
```

```cpp
    delete root;
    return 0;
}
```

14.4 Behavioral Patterns

Observer Pattern

The Observer pattern defines a one-to-many dependency between objects, allowing one object (the subject) to notify multiple observers about changes in its state. This is useful for implementing event-driven systems.

Example:
cpp

```cpp
#include <iostream>
#include <vector>
using namespace std;

class Observer {
public:
    virtual void update(int state) = 0; // Observer interface
};
```

```cpp
class Subject {
private:
    vector<Observer*> observers;
    int state;

public:
    void attach(Observer* observer) {
        observers.push_back(observer); // Attaching an observer
    }

    void setState(int newState) {
        state = newState;
        notify(); // Notify all observers
    }

    void notify() {
        for (Observer* observer : observers) {
            observer->update(state); // Updating all observers
        }
    }
};

class ConcreteObserver : public Observer {
```

```cpp
public:
    void update(int state) override {
        cout << "Observer notified with state: " << state << endl; // Handling state update
    }
};

int main() {
    Subject* subject = new Subject();
    ConcreteObserver* observer1 = new ConcreteObserver();
    ConcreteObserver* observer2 = new ConcreteObserver();

    subject->attach(observer1);
    subject->attach(observer2);

    subject->setState(10); // Changing state and notifying observers

    delete observer1;
    delete observer2;
    delete subject;
    return 0;
}
```

Strategy Pattern

The Strategy pattern defines a family of algorithms, encapsulating each one and making them interchangeable. This pattern lets the algorithm vary independently from clients that use it.

Example:

cpp

```cpp
#include <iostream>
using namespace std;

class Strategy {
public:
    virtual void execute() = 0; // Strategy interface
};

class ConcreteStrategyA : public Strategy {
public:
    void execute() override {
        cout << "Executing Strategy A" << endl; // Concrete strategy A
    }
};
```

```cpp
class ConcreteStrategyB : public Strategy {
public:
   void execute() override {
      cout << "Executing Strategy B" << endl; // Concrete strategy B
   }
};

class Context {
private:
   Strategy* strategy;

public:
   void setStrategy(Strategy* newStrategy) {
      strategy = newStrategy; // Setting strategy
   }

   void executeStrategy() {
      strategy->execute();   // Executing current strategy
   }
};

int main() {
   Context* context = new Context();
```

```cpp
    ConcreteStrategyA* strategyA = new ConcreteStrategyA();
    ConcreteStrategyB* strategyB = new ConcreteStrategyB();

    context->setStrategy(strategyA);
    context->executeStrategy(); // Using strategy A

    context->setStrategy(strategyB);
    context->executeStrategy(); // Using strategy B

    delete strategyA;
    delete strategyB;
    delete context;
    return 0;
}
```

14.5 Conclusion

Design patterns play a significant role in software development, providing standardized solutions to common problems. In this chapter, we explored various design patterns in C++, including:

Creational Patterns: Singleton and Factory patterns for object creation.

Structural Patterns: Adapter and Composite patterns for object composition.

Behavioral Patterns: Observer and Strategy patterns for managing object interactions.

By applying these design patterns, you can write cleaner, more efficient, and more maintainable code. Understanding and utilizing design patterns will enhance your ability to design robust, scalable applications in C++.

Chapter 15: Best Practices for Object-Oriented Programming in C++

Object-Oriented Programming (OOP) is a powerful programming paradigm that enables developers to create modular, reusable, and maintainable code. However, writing good object-oriented code requires adherence to certain best practices. In this final chapter, we will explore key best practices for OOP in C++, focusing on principles that enhance code quality, maintainability, and performance.

15.1 Follow the SOLID Principles

The SOLID principles are five design principles intended to make software designs more understandable, flexible, and maintainable:

Single Responsibility Principle (SRP): A class should have only one reason to change, meaning it should have only one job or responsibility. This promotes low coupling and high cohesion. **Example**:

```cpp
class Report {
public:
    void generateReport() {
        // Generate report logic
    }
};

class ReportPrinter {
public:
    void printReport(const Report& report) {
        // Print report logic
    }
};
```

Open/Closed Principle (OCP): Classes should be open for extension but closed for modification. You can achieve this through inheritance and interfaces.

Example:
```cpp
class Shape {
```

```cpp
public:
    virtual double area() const = 0;
};

class Circle : public Shape {
public:
    double area() const override {
        // Circle area calculation
        return 3.14 * radius * radius;
    }
};

class Rectangle : public Shape {
public:
    double area() const override {
        // Rectangle area calculation
        return width * height;
    }
};
```

Liskov Substitution Principle (LSP): Subtypes must be substitutable for their base types without altering the correctness of the program. This ensures that derived classes extend the behavior of the base class without changing its expected behavior.

Interface Segregation Principle (ISP): Clients should not be forced to depend on interfaces they do not use. This principle advocates for smaller, more specific interfaces rather than a large, general-purpose interface.

Dependency Inversion Principle (DIP): High-level modules should not depend on low-level modules but on abstractions. This reduces coupling between different parts of the application.

15.2 Use Encapsulation Wisely

Encapsulation is the practice of restricting access to certain components of an object and exposing only what is necessary. This improves security and reduces dependencies between objects.

Access Modifiers: Use `public`, `protected`, and `private` access specifiers to control the visibility of class members.

Example:

cpp

```cpp
class BankAccount {
private:
    double balance;

public:
    BankAccount(double initialBalance) : balance(initialBalance) {}

    void deposit(double amount) {
        if (amount > 0) {
            balance += amount;
        }
    }

    double getBalance() const {
        return balance; // Only exposing necessary information
    }
};
```

15.3 Prefer Composition Over Inheritance

While inheritance is a key feature of OOP, it can lead to tight coupling and complicated hierarchies. Prefer composition, where a class is composed of one or more objects of other classes, to achieve flexibility and reuse.

Example:

cpp

```cpp
class Engine {
public:
   void start() {
      // Engine start logic
   }
};

class Car {
private:
   Engine engine; // Composition

public:
   void start() {
      engine.start(); // Delegating start to the Engine
   }
};
```

15.4 Implement Proper Error Handling

Robust error handling is critical for maintaining application stability. Use exceptions to handle errors gracefully, as discussed in Chapter 13.

Throw Exceptions: Use `throw` to signal an error condition.

Catch Exceptions: Handle exceptions using `try-catch` blocks to prevent crashes and maintain program flow.

15.5 Write Clean and Readable Code

Clean code is essential for maintaining and extending your software. Here are some guidelines:

Consistent Naming Conventions: Use meaningful variable, function, and class names that convey their purpose. Stick to a naming convention throughout your codebase.

Example:

cpp

```
class UserProfile {
public:
    void updateProfile(const std::string& username, const std::string& email);
};
```

Commenting and Documentation: Write comments to explain complex logic and document public interfaces to make the code easier to understand.

Limit Class and Function Size: Keep classes and functions small, focusing on a single responsibility. This enhances readability and maintainability.

15.6 Utilize RAII (Resource Acquisition Is Initialization)

RAII is a programming idiom that ensures resource management through object lifetime. By tying resource allocation and deallocation to object lifespan, you prevent memory leaks and resource mismanagement.

Example:

cpp

```cpp
#include <iostream>
#include <memory>
using namespace std;

class Resource {
public:
    Resource() {
        cout << "Resource acquired." << endl;
    }
    ~Resource() {
        cout << "Resource released." << endl;
    }
};

void useResource() {
    unique_ptr<Resource> res = make_unique<Resource>(); // RAII in action
```

```cpp
    // Resource is automatically released when 'res'
goes out of scope
}

int main() {
    useResource();
    return 0;
}
```

15.7 Conduct Thorough Testing

Testing is essential for ensuring the correctness and reliability of your code. Write unit tests to validate individual components, and consider using automated testing frameworks like Google Test.

Test-Driven Development (TDD): Consider adopting TDD, where you write tests before implementing the corresponding code. This approach helps clarify requirements and reduces defects.

15.8 Conclusion

In this final chapter, we explored key best practices for Object-Oriented Programming in C++, including:

SOLID Principles: Essential design principles for creating maintainable and scalable systems.

Encapsulation: Protecting object state and providing controlled access.

Composition over Inheritance: Favoring composition for flexibility and reuse.

Error Handling: Implementing robust exception handling mechanisms.

Clean Code: Writing readable and maintainable code.

RAII: Managing resources effectively through object lifetimes.

Testing: Ensuring correctness through thorough testing practices.

By following these best practices, you can develop high-quality C++ applications that are robust, scalable, and easier to maintain. Embracing these principles will enhance your programming skills and help you become a more effective software developer.

www.ingramcontent.com/pod-product-compliance
Lightning Source LLC
Chambersburg PA
CBHW052150220526
45471CB00004B/1617